Tarot for

Beginners

The 143 Pages In-Depth Yet
Comprehensive Guide to Master
Tarot divination, history, usage and
modern decks for a Newbie or an
Intermediate Level Tarot User;
Become a Tarot Expert in Less
Than 72 hours

Part-2

By

Kira Glent

Table of Contents

complete information. No warranties of any kind are declared or implied. Readers acknowledge that the author is not engaging in the rendering of legal, financial, medical or professional advice. The content within this book has been derived from various sources. Please consult a licensed professional before attempting any techniques outlined in this book.

By reading this document, the reader agrees that under no circumstances is the author responsible for any losses, direct or indirect, which are incurred as a result of the use of information contained within this document, including, but not limited to, — errors, omissions, or inaccuracies.

Tarot for Beginners

Introduction

What is Card game?

A game is any game utilizing playing a card game as the essential gadget with which the game is played, be they customary or game-explicit.

Innumerable games exist, including groups of related games, (for example, poker). Few games played with customary decks have officially institutionalized standards, however most are society games whose rules shift by district, culture, and individual.

A game is played with a deck or pack of playing a game of cards which are indistinguishable fit as a fiddle. Each card has different sides, the face and the back. Regularly the backs of the cards are vague. The essences of the cards may all be one of a kind, or there can be copies. The piece of a deck is known to every player. At times a few decks are rearranged together to shape a solitary pack or shoe.

Games utilizing playing a game of cards abuse the way that cards are exclusively recognizable from one side just, so every player knows just the cards he holds and not those held by any other person. Therefore games are regularly portrayed as rounds of possibility or "flawed data"— as particular from rounds of procedure or "immaculate data," where the present position is completely unmistakable to all players all through the game. Many games that are not commonly put in the group of games do in truth use cards for some part of their ongoing interaction.

A few games that are set in the game sort include a board. The differentiation is that the interactivity of a game mainly relies upon the utilization of the cards by players (the board is just a guide for scorekeeping or for card arrangement), while table games (the head non game sort to utilize cards) for the most part center around the players' situations on the board, and utilize the cards for some auxiliary reason.

Game, game played for joy or betting (or both) with at least one decks of playing a game of cards. Games utilizing playing a game of cards misuse the way that cards are independently recognizable from one side just, with the goal that every player knows just the cards he holds and not those held by any other individual.

Consequently games are frequently described as rounds of possibility or "blemished data"— as unmistakable from rounds of methodology or "impeccable data," where the present position is completely obvious to all players all through the game. This portrayal is lacking, in any case. For instance, in backgammon, a bones game, the beginning position is foreordained and equivalent, and every single ensuing move are completely known to the two players. What comprises the blemish of its data is the unusualness of future bones rolls. Shakers games are in this manner rounds of future defective data since whatever key expertise they involve must be founded on an evaluation of future occasions, mainly through the arithmetic of likelihood hypothesis. Interestingly, the possibility component of games is a consequence of rearranging the cards before play so as to randomize their underlying dissemination. From that point, dexterous play to a great extent comprises of deciding the appropriation of cards through perception, which, contingent upon the game, may incorporate perception of players' offers, disposes of, and stunt play. Games are in this manner rounds of "past blemished data" or, all the more essentially, expanding data. This isn't to attest that all games are scholarly or even interest a lot of ability. There are even games where every one of the cards are managed faceup, particularly assortments of solitaire, which makes them rounds of flawless data.

Roots

Inborn proof recommends that a stunt taking game with no exceptional suit, or trump suit, alongside playing a game of cards, arrived at Europe in the fourteenth century, likely by entry through the Islamic world. The soonest game known by name—karnöffel, played from 1428 in Germany—was such, however certain cards of a haphazardly chosen suit had stunt taking forces of fluctuating degrees of prevalence. Trump suits all things considered were an European development (see tarot game), just like the consequent thought of offering to choose a trump suit (see hombre). Betting rounds of the point -check, or blackjack, type, known from the fifteenth century, may have been gotten from dice games, as they disregard any differentiation between suits. Betting rounds of the competing, or poker, type are known from the sixteenth century, as is noddy, the progenitor of cribbage. Some supposed kids' games, for example, poor person my-neighbor and old house keeper, get from old drinking and betting games. Different groups of games, especially non-stunt taking games, arrived at Europe from the Far East, particularly from China. They incorporate the club family (seventeenth century), the rummy family (nineteenth century), which likely got from mah-jongg, and the president family (twentieth century).

Qualities

The ubiquity of cards as gaming materials gets from a remarkable blend of attributes:

Get select access to content from our 1768 First Edition with your membership.

Buy in today

Cards are little, effectively compact, and outwardly appealing.

Cards effectively loan themselves to the improvement of a wide range of games, and varieties inside given games, fit to various abilities and demeanors.

Reasonable games can be found for a particular number of players from one to twelve. They likewise give the choice of playing as people against each other, in fixed associations (as in connect), or in specially appointed organizations from arrangement to bargain (as in solo whist and call-pro euchre).

Games are normally quick, comprising of various arrangements that last just a couple of moments each. This supports the sharp, manages visit open doors for verbal associating (among bargains), and, for card sharks, encourages quick inversions of fortune.

They produce more changed and fascinating scores than basic "win-lose-draw."

A portion of these highlights identify with the betting capability of games, however a steady perspective on cards as betting games is both old fashioned and unreasonable. An inborn betting game is one in which players can apply no power over the result, so the main maintainable enthusiasm for playing lies in the rush or dread of winning or losing cash. Obviously, any game can be played for cash, however a few games, for example, scaffold or chess, offer adequate mental compensations to keep up players' enthusiasm for lieu of any budgetary motivator.

Order

Most Western games are stunt games, in which every player thusly plays a card to the table, and whoever plays the best card wins them all. These cards comprise a stunt, which the victor places face down in a heap before playing the main card to the following stunt. The best card is typically the most noteworthy positioning card of a similar suit as the card drove—that is, of a similar suit as the principal card played to the stunt. Any individual who neglects to take action accordingly to the card drove can't win the stunt, regardless of how high the card.

Winning a stunt is doubly favorable, since the player who wins a stunt increases material as well as picks which suit to lead straightaway. A player who drives a suit that nobody can follow (in light of the fact that nobody else has any cards of that suit left) wins that stunt paying little mind to card rank.

Stunt play can be changed in a few different ways. The most critical is by some procedure of assigning one of the four suits as an exceptional trump suit, better in power than the other three suits. By and large, this empowers a player who is out of whatever suit was directed to take advantage of an ace in the hole rather, a demonstration known as besting or ruffing, which will beat any cards of the suit drove.

Stunt games might be subdivided as follows:

Plain-stunt games. The point is to win however many deceives as could be expected under the circumstances (as in whist or spades) or if nothing else the same number of stunts as offer (extension, euchre) or (infrequently) precisely the quantity of stunts offer (goodness hellfire! ninety-nine).

Point-stunt games. To win the best estimation of point-scoring cards contained in stunts (scat, each of the fours, tarot games).

Stunt shirking games. To abstain from winning punishment cards contained in stunts (hearts) or winning any stunts whatsoever (misère).

Stunt and-merge games. To make merges (card blends) notwithstanding winning stunts or card-focuses contained in stunts (piquet, bezique, pinochle, sixty-six).

Games dependent on standards other than stunt taking include:

Catching games. The point is to gather or catch cards by techniques other than stunt taking (club, slap jack, goops, snap, homeless person my-neighbor, fight). Many—yet in no way, shape or form all—are kids' games.

Including games. A running complete is kept of the presumptive estimations of cards played to the table, and the point is to make or abstain from making certain aggregates. Cribbage, the most modern model, additionally incorporates card blends.

Shedding games. The point is either to be the first to play out the entirety of one's cards (insane eights, Michigan, New market, president) or to abstain from being the last player staying with a card or cards close by (old house cleaner).

Merging or rummy games. The point is either to be the first out of cards by merging them all in substantial blends (gin rummy) or to make and score however many merges as could reasonably be expected before going out (canasta, samba).

Solitaire or persistence games. One-player games, the point typically being to set the rearranged deck all together (canfield, Klondike). Focused patience's for more than one player (dashing evil presence, jump, dislike and malevolence) become, in actuality, shedding or merging games.

Competing games. Gifted betting games where players compete with each other about who holds the best card mix or is probably going to complete with the best when their hands are finished (poker, boast).

Banking games. Less-talented betting games where players wager on having or securing preferred cards over the seller or financier (baccarat, blackjack). Most are gambling club games, the investor being an agent of the administration. In home play, players may adjust their odds by alternating as the investor.

Staking games. Incompetent betting games where players essentially wager on specific cards' turning up (faro, trended-et-quartet).

Tarot Card Reading:

Tarot card perusing is the act of utilizing tarot cards to pick up knowledge into the past, present or future by defining an inquiry, at that point drawing and deciphering cards. Perusing tarot cards is a sort of cartomancy.

A tarot perusing gives you direction for your relationship, your profession, and some other part of your life. Be that as it may, a solid tarot peruser isn't constantly accessible immediately. Fortunately, there are various tarot spreads you can do without anyone else.

This 3-card individual perusing spread answers inquiries concerning your past, present, and future. As you select your 3 cards, consider the inquiries you'd like replied or the issues you're confronting. As you read the understandings on each card, think about how they apply to the inquiry you posed or your present circumstance.

The first Card (The Past): This card speaks to your circumstance—why you're right now in the spot you're in. It frequently symbolizes an individual or relationship in your life that has affected your inquiry.

The second Card (The Present): This card speaks to the present issue, frequently as an immediate aftereffect of the circumstance. Give close consideration to this card as it might be attempting to give you things that you've recently disregarded.

The third Card (The Future): The last card in this 3-card spread gives direction to confront and beat your issue. It might give choices you hadn't considered or assets and individuals you'd neglected.

Subsequent to drawing your cards, return to your underlying inquiry to guarantee that it has been tended to appropriately. A decent tarot guide can assist you with interpretting the pictures you see on the tarot cards, however there's actually not a viable alternative for individual reflection. Similarly as with any ability, careful discipline brings about promising results, so utilize this tarot apparatus frequently (day by day, if conceivable), or request a lot of Astrology Answers Master Deck Tarot Cards and practice at home!

On the 2 of Pentacles, we see a figure shuffling 2 coins, the endlessness image integrating the coins.

There is a feeling of compromise in this card, and that could be profoundly, inwardly, or monetarily. You might be shuffling a great deal of bills at this moment, or a ton of messages identified with affection. You might be conflicted between sweethearts, or another person may be. You may likewise be shuffling a couple of various occupations to bring home the bacon when this card shows up.

The 2 of Pentacles is a transient card and a phase card, implying that the dark line isolating the front from the back in this image is revealing to you that not all things are as it appears. Simultaneously, being a transient card or Minor Arcana, we realize this isn't an actual existence shaking thing. Yet at the same time. That karma. The exercise in careful control you are in right currently won't keep going forever, yet you do should be reasonable with all gatherings. You might be seeing a great deal of desk work going to and fro today in work, business, or land. Be that as it may, you may likewise be imparting to and fro in an adoration circumstance.

Perfect partners, life mates, twin blazes, twin beams, holy agreements, karmic joins, related spirits—it's anything but difficult to get confounded about what they mean.The tarot can give a wonderful look at how this association is unfurling, and you don't should be a card master to dive into things, either. We've done that for you! All you have to do now is to concentrate on your inquiry. We'll bargain the cards for you for a tarot love perusing and present you with a preview of knowledge concerning what's up 'til now inconspicuous.

First Position: Do Our Souls Already Know Each Other

The card in this position gives you a look at what your concurrence with one another may be. It's a paradox that everybody you meet is some awesome association. That doesn't imply that there's no reason for them in your life. It's uncommon to meet somebody your spirit definitely knows, and when you do, well, this tart card can be a sign that you have to give close consideration to that association. It isn't generally hearts and blossoms, however. At times those connections from your past are a test, to perceive how far you've come and the amount you have developed. Few out of every odd soul association is cherishing, or even kind. Now and then a spirit that you definitely know comes to you as an instructor, and only one out of every odd exercise is one that is wonderful or simple to learn.

Second Position: Should I Invest My Time in This Relationship

Regardless of whether a relationship isn't intended to be dependable or submitted, it may in any case merit your time! What would you be able to gain from it? By what method will it empower you to develop? These are significant inquiries, questions that this card in your tarot love perusing may reply. Putting your time in the relationship implies that you're willing to open yourself to divine vitality and experience whatever experience you're intended to have. You have through and through freedom. You can retreat from a promising exercise, or you can go directly into something that isn't proper. The cards will encourage you what to do, yet by the day's end, it's dependent upon you to settle on the choice, and live with any results—positive or negative—of the way you picked.

Third Position: How Does the Future of This Relationship Look

Ok, presently we're finding a good pace coarse. This tarot card, in this position, gives you a trace of what's yet to come. Obviously, numerous elements play into this, and on the off chance that you do this perusing, and afterward do it again quickly you could get an altogether extraordinary outcome. Why? Since the principal perusing gave you some information, it changed your mindfulness. Everything gets into quantum material science, you'll simply need to confide in me on this one. Regardless of whether this is a consummately positive card, it doesn't imply that this relationship is a match made in heaven. All connections must be dealt with. On the off chance that you're both not going to contribute equivalent insightfulness, regard, and thought, at that point things could in any case self-destruct. What's more, don't stress excessively if this is a negative card. It doesn't imply that your relationship is damned. It implies that there's work to do if it will last and flourish. Is it true that you are both ready to put forth the attempt?

Tarot Gaming Deck:

Decks intended to play games, for example, track.

Alan Tarot

The Alan Tarot Deck has 78 cards in the track style. The majors and courts have twofold finished, fascinating craftsmanship deco style outlines made by Orell in 1910, while the numbered suit cards are basic playing a game of cards.

Erde Track

The Erde Track (or Tarot of the Earth) is a Marseilles-based deck with solid, individual, and reversable drawings. Distributed in a marked and restricted release of 500 duplicates.

Omegaland

Omegaland is a 78 card deck set in a tragic, prophetically catastrophic present day universe of a similar name. The outlines are survivalist and substantial on the rifles, crossbows, and tins of beans. It's both a tarot deck and game, and directions for both are incorporated with the deck.

Tarot Asterix

The Tarot Asterix highlights characters and scenes from Asterix, the outstanding French comic, on its twofold finished cards. While named a Tarot, this is a deck proposed for the round of Track, as opposed to divination or direction.

Tarot of Loka

The Tarot of Loka is a family game set in the dreamland of Loka, showed by Ralph Horsley and planned by Alessio Cavatore. The deck is motivated by medieval tarot and gives recognition to tarot's causes as a game. It very well may be utilized for the Tarot of Loka game, as a tarot deck, or as a playing card set.

Tarot Philatelique

The Tarot Philatelique (or Philatelic Tarot) is a French deck intended to play the round of Tarot, instead of for readings. The majors and court cards include French stamps and the minors are fundamentally the same as playing a card game.

Trionfi: Tarot Playing Cards

Trionfi: Tarot Playing Cards is a lot of 78 Anglo-American playing a game of cards, intended for English speakers to play the Tarot, Track and Tarocchi rounds of mainland Europe. The cards are twofold finished and have symbolism dependent on nineteenth century European tarots.

Heavenly attendant Tarot Decks

Heavenly attendant tarot decks and prophet cards depend on holy messengers or radiant creatures.

Heavenly attendant Answers Oracle

The Angel Answers Oracle is a 44-card deck for straightforward, clear and unambiguous counsel. The cards have beautiful representations of holy messengers in addition to direct exhortation at the base of the card. The deck can be utilized alone or to improve readings with different decks.

Blessed messenger Dreams Oracle

The Angel Dreams Oracle is a 55-card deck for dream translation and comprehension from Doreen

Virtue. The cards portray a wide scope of genuine and dream subjects (instead of just holy messengers) and give solid, positive guidance

Holy messenger Insight Pack

The Angel Insight Pack is a prophet deck with holy messenger symbolism intended to give motivation, knowledge and direction. The 52 cards have silver features and show singular blessed messengers (not named) with a catchphrase at the base of the card.

Heavenly attendant Inspiration Oracle

The Angel Inspiration Oracle is intended to help stir the peruser to the heavenly attendants around them. The 44 card outlines are hand-drawn and joined by a watchword. Each deck is accessible from and assembled by the craftsman.

Blessed messenger Love Cards

The Angel Love Cards tell the client the best way to channel the intensity of the adoration holy messengers, through 40 huge size cards and their related statements, petitions and activities. This deck isn't intended for readings, however for the drawing of a solitary card for reflection, consideration and direction.

Blessed messenger Oracle Open

The Angel Oracle has 36 shown blessed messenger cards partitioned into three chains of command of paradise: structure, creation, and heaven. There are chief heavenly messengers, domains and excellencies, individual blessed messengers and more on the yellow-darker shaded cards.

Blessed messenger Prayers Oracle

The Angel Prayers Oracle is a cutting edge take on blessed messengers and lead celestial hosts, and the intelligence and mending they can give. The 44 cards have contemporary pictures of heavenly attendants from varying backgrounds, and certifiable petitions connected with the message of each card.

Blessed messenger Tarot

The Tarot de los Angeles is a Spanish-distributed deck, with 78 cards and a bizarre structure identifying with the gatherings of heavenly attendants, lead celestial hosts, faeries, dwarves and seraphim.

Blessed messenger Tarot

The Angel Tarot has animation representations of generally female heavenly attendants set over pictures of planets and the universe. The minor arcana are not grand and have brightened pips set over comparable space symbolism. The titles on the enormous white fringes are in a few dialects.

Holy messenger Tarot

The Angel Tarot is a bright 78-card deck, generally dependent on the Rider-Waite establishment. The cards are hand-drawn pencil representations, planned to enable the peruser to take advantage of their instinct and tweak their association with their heavenly attendants.

Heavenly attendant Tarot Cards

The Angel Tarot Cards is the principal tarot from the exceptionally famous maker of prophet decks, Doreen Virtue. It's a full arrangement of 78 cards with pictures of holy messengers, mermaids, unicorns and pixies, intended to be '100 percent delicate, safe, and reliable'. It's a basic and simple to utilize prologue to tarot cards.

Holy messenger Therapy Oracle Cards

The Angel Therapy Oracle Cards is one of the numerous decks from Doreen Virtue. This one is committed to the chief heavenly messengers and gatekeeper holy messengers, and has 44 cards with other-worldly pictures and obscure messages on each card.

Blessed messenger Voices Oracle

A truly, clean 80-card prophet dependent on the customary Christian watchman heavenly attendants and lead celestial hosts. The Angel Voices Oracle likewise consolidates prophetic affiliations, appeared by the shading coding of the heavenly attendants' experiences and garments.

Holy messengers of Abundance Oracle Cards

Holy messengers of Abundance is a 44-card prophet deck from Doreen Virtue and her child, Grant Virtue. This deck is intended to help tap into an attitude of success and potential, and away from need and neediness, through direction from the blessed messengers.

Heavenly attendants of Atlantis Oracle

The Angels of Atlantis has 44 cards of astronomical montage symbolism, themed around the lessons of the 12 lead celestial hosts of Atlantis. It's intended to offer direction and mending, and 'a profound association with the old domain of Atlantis'.

Blessed messengers Tarot

Blessed messengers from the Christian pantheon are highlighted on the major arcana cards, ilustrating in Robert Place's mark style. The minor arcana of the Angel Tarot are plain with just the proper images, for example, eight hearts, or two precious stones.

Heavenly attendants, Gods and Goddesses Oracle cards

The Angels, Gods, and Goddesses Oracle Cards are another from Toni Carmine Salerno, this deck concentrating on original energies as opposed to explicit strict divinities. Each card has a brilliant canvas and otherworldly exhortation at the base of the card. Bundled in tough cardboard case with a 64 -page friend booklet.

Lead celestial host Oracle cards

The Archangel Oracle Cards include 15 blessed messengers from different religions and customs more than 45 cards. The best 66% of each card has an appealing blessed messenger ilustration, while the lower third has the card's title and guidance from its chief heavenly messenger. This set by Doreen Virtue is a famous one for individuals who have never utilized Tarot cards.

Chief heavenly messenger Power Tarot

The Archangel Power Tarot is the second invasion into tarot by exceptionally famous New Age creator, Doreen Virtue. This intensely changed deck highlights Photoshopped, collaged craftsmanship that extents from dream to medieval to current, with a pretty lead celestial host and a positive message on each card.

Lead celestial host Raphael Healing Oracle Cards

Lead celestial host Raphael Healing Oracle Cards is a deck from Doreen Virtue and has 44 cards, each with an artistic creation of the heavenly attendant Raphael. The deck is intended for wellbeing and recuperating readings, or to stir your own mending capacities.

Ask an Angel Oracle Cards

The 42 Ask an Angel cards have an assortment of pretty pictures, with customary people, winged people, and winged animals all creation an appearance. Each card records the name of the heavenly attendant or lead celestial host, and a watchword.

Ask Angels Oracle Cards

The Ask Angels Oracle Cards has 44 lovely and elevating cards made by creator and blessed messenger channel, Melanie Beckler. It was structured so you can without much of a stretch get blessed messenger messages and direction, and is a computerized just deck. Accessible on the Ask

Angels site or as an application.

Brassy Action Angels Oracle

The AAA Oracle - Audacious Action Angels Oracle - is an instrument to interface you with your blessed messengers for fast and clear counsel. It has some good times and particular cards each with its very own profound message - from the Direct Dial Archangel to the 3 Wishes and the News Flash.

Blue Angel Oracle

The Blue Angel Oracle has 45 elevating cards of direction and astuteness. It's themed around the Archangel Michael, also called the 'Blue Angel', and has extraordinary, dynamic symbolism.

Day by day Guidance from Your Angels Oracle Cards

The Daily Guidance from Your Angels Oracle Cards is the ninth prophet deck from Doreen Virtue. This deck has lovely cards highlighting blessed messengers in the top half, and a divinatory subject and informative section in the lower half.

Dim Angels Tarot

The Dark Angels Tarot is a gothic tarot concentrating on paradise's outsider heavenly attendants. "Painfully delightful, baffling, and without a doubt shrewd, these absurd animals have a lot to show us of our own shadow selves."

Devas of Creation

The Devas of Creation is a 72-card prophet deck for working with the Devas, the multi-dimensional energies or 'Sparkling Ones', as portrayed by Sanskrit spiritualists. The 72 cards move from The Void, Divinity and the Angelic Realms through to The Planets, The Seasons and Earth situations and are intended for numerous utilizations - contemplation, treatment, or working through negative energies.

Gatekeeper Angel Cards

The heart-molded cards of the Guardian Angel
Cards are from productive craftsman, Toni Carmine
Salerno. The 44 cards have no photos, only a
watchword and a rousing passage or supplication on
a shaded foundation. Bundled with a 46-page buddy

booklet.

Gatekeeper Angel Tarot Cards

The Guardian Angel Tarot Cards is a tarot deck for the 'profoundly delicate' from New Age creator, Doreen Virtue, which proceeds with the delicate and sweet topic of her prior decks. Every one of the 78 gold-edged, rearranged cards includes a heavenly attendant representation and a positive clarification printed underneath.

Watchman Tarot

The Guardian Tarot is a blessed messenger themed, gothic deck dependent on Rider-Waite imagery. Autonomously distributed.

Recuperating Light and Angel Cards

The Healing Light and Angel Cards has 42 cards isolated into (and utilized as) six distinct segments: Chakras, Action, Color, Animals, Crystals and Angels. The deck is intended to help distinguish and afterward recuperate blocked chakras.

Mending with the Angels Oracle

44 cards of in an unexpected way styled holy messenger pictures with multi-shaded outskirts. Each card in the Healing with the Angels Oracle represents a characteristic or movement, for example, Listening, Forgiveness, or Spiritual Growth.

Dull and Gothic Tarot Decks

Dull and gothic Tarot cards and decks, including vampires, shadows, and extraordinary dreams. These Tarot decks center around the darker side of life and creative mind.

Appalling Tarot

The Abysmal Tarot is another other option, workmanship tarot with a sinister topic. It is a quality set with 22 cards by ten unique specialists, each including a Devil or devilish viewpoint. Distributed in a constrained release of 333 duplicates, with 22 of these decks having an additional card called Abigor.

Catalytic Wedding Tarot

The Alchemical Wedding Tarot is a to some degree dim deck with an extraordinary, dream-like quality. The sepia-conditioned craftsmanship was made from arrangement composed on PC, including solid symbolism of individuals showing up in covers and semi-creature structures. The 22-card restricted release is currently sold out.

Speculative chemistry 1977 England Tarot

The Alchemy 1977 England Tarot is a darker tarot with a frightfulness edge. A considerable lot of the scenes on the majors include smiling skeletons, while the court have a dull dream feel. The minor arcana don't have scenes, however the suit components are finished to fit the subject.

All Hallow's Tarot

The All Hallow's Tarot is an advanced, Halloween-themed workmanship tarot of 22 cards, highlighting goths, apparitions, punks, mediums and then some. It's been independently published in a constrained release run of 50 decks with little size, covered cards. Presently likewise accessible in an entire 78 card version.

All Hallows Tarot

The All Hallows Tarot, already just accessible in a 22 card set, is a presently full 79 card deck (the standard 78 in addition to a Happy Squirrel card). It has a cutting edge Halloween topic, with unusual individuals rising up out of the dull - goths, phantoms, punks and mediums - attracted Robyn's trademark style.

Animalis os Fortuna Tarot

The Animalis os Fortuna Tarot is a grotesque yet not violent 78-card highly contrasting tarot deck that utilizations creatures and issues that remains to be worked out each card. Each major arcana card includes an alternate creature and the suits have additionally been adjusted to the collective of animals. The deck is independently published by the creator.

Anne Stokes Gothic Tarot

Anne Stokes Gothic Tarot is a 78-card deck from a similar craftsman as the Necronomicon Tarot. The cards are loaded up with a dim dream blend of winged serpents, unicorns, skulls, vampires and bats. The minor arcana cards simply show masterminded suit components, as opposed to delineated scenes.

Anne Stokes Legends Tarot

The Anne Stokes Legends Tarot is a 78-card tarot deck with outlines browsed crafted by the productive dream craftsman of a similar name. The deck is beautiful in a smooth sentimental medieval style, yet just approximately connected with tarot imagery. The minor arcana are likewise pip cards as opposed to being completely represented scenes.

Archeon Tarot

The Archeon Tarot includes a blend of customary and non-conventional symbolism in dream-like computerized montage, motivated by the creator's close to home imagery and folklore.

Barbieri Tarot

The Barbieri Tarot is an energetic, effectively delineated 78 card deck from Italian craftsman and ace of the dream classification, Paolo Barbieri. Choices of his dim, searing and point by point workmanship have been decided to fit the tarot paradigms.

Dark Tarot

The Black Tarot is an exploratory arrangement of theoretical shading collections made on dark foundations. Just seven cards have been finished up until now.

Dark Tarot

The Black Tarot is a dim gothic dream deck by comic book craftsman Luis Royo. It is intended to be utilized for investigating the darker side of the mind. Presently likewise accessible in a completely shown form as the Royo Dark Tarot.

Bohemian Gothic Tarot

The Bohemian Gothic Tarot is the dull sister of the Victorian Romantic Tarot. It's a deck of the shadows; dull, lovely, somewhat despairing and baffling. The releases of the deck and a deck-and-book set are presently no longer available.

Book of Kaos Tarot

The Book of Kaos Tarot is a convincing independently published 80-card deck. The symbolism utilizes agnostic and ancestral symbolism and its pen-and-ink craftsmanship shifts from easy to complex over the cards.

Bosch Tarots

Strikingly dynamic, the Bosch Tarot deck delineates people, beasts, and dreams as Tarot cards. The workmanship style is displayed on that of Dutch craftsman Hieronymous Bosch and has components from his canvases. Captivating.

Corneal Edema Tarot

The Corneal Edema Tarot is a craftsmanship tarot praising the gothic way of life. The pictures are made out of presented photos, graphically altered to install them into a finished space. The 22 majors have now been distributed in a constrained release of 50 decks.

Crow's Magick Tarot

The Crow's Magick Tarot is the subsequent deck made by craftsman Londa. The cards have an exceptionally dim feel, presumably on the grounds that the greater part of the scenes have a dark foundation. I don't know how the images identify with conventional tarot, however the pictures are amazing.

Remorseless Thing Tarot

The Cruel Thing Tarot is a hazily exquisite gothic tarot deck, printed altogether in dark, white and red. The minors aren't completely beautiful however have more enthusiasm than plain pips.

Daemon Tarot

The Daemon Tarot is a 69-card divination deck drawing upon The Infernal Dictionary, a nineteenth century assortment of daemon legend. The deck joins 69 daemons and their characteristics with each card, and helps with getting to their energies.

Dim Angels Tarot

The Dark Angels Tarot is a gothic tarot concentrating on paradise's untouchable heavenly attendants. "Painfully wonderful, puzzling, and without a doubt shrewd, these ridiculous animals have a lot to show us of our own shadow selves."

Dim Carnival Tarot

The Dark Carnival Tarot is based around dim bazaar symbolism, roused by the juggalo subculture and melodic type in America. The 78 cards have a customary premise, outlined with a urban spray painting feel.

Dim Fairytale Tarot

The Dark Fairytale Tarot is an investigation of the darker side of the universe of the fae. It takes components of both the Rider-Waite and Thoth establishments and mixes them with exact medieval dream symbolism.

Dim Goddess Tarot

The Dark Goddess Tarot highlights 78 goddesses and legendary ladies, figures who may be viewed as dim, shadow or testing. The reasonable, striking workmanship is outwardly predictable, yet remains consistent with every goddess' birthplaces. It's a profound and well-made deck, independently published in a constrained version of 1000 duplicates.

Dim Grimoire Tarot

The Dark Grimoire Tarot takes its motivation from mystical writings of fiction and legend - the Necronomicon and different grimoires. The 78 cards have non-conventional scenes of ghastliness and bad dream. Frequently abnormal, they're additionally in some cases upsetting, especially in the strict Hanged Man.

Darkana Tarot

The Darkana Tarot "consolidates a cutting edge grunge style with non-conventional tarot imagery". It's an entire 79-card deck from the maker of the Inappropriate Tarot Readings gathering, with an additional major arcana card - the Badass.

Deck of the Dead

The Deck of the Dead has 78 cards made from vintage etchings and prints, all themed around Death. Each card has been altered to fit the Rider-Waite framework and the minors are completely outlined. Independently published by the craftsman, it's accessible in three unique sizes.

Degenerate Moon Tarot

The Deviant Moon Tarot has dreamlike, extremely one of a kind, and in some cases upsetting twilight work of art. It's enlivened by (and joins) pictures of cemetaries and mental refuges, and intended to light up further pieces of the subsconscious. The gifted artist is additionally a tarot understudy, and the deck is the aftereffect of three years of aesthetic work. Presently additionally accessible in a borderless version.

Journal of a Broken Soul

The Diary of a Broken Soul Tarot, a carefully gothic highly contrasting deck, is the appearance of craftsman Ash's shadow work. Presently independently published in a 78 card release, there is likewise a marginally extraordinary 22 card version.

Journal of a Broken Soul Tarot

The Diary of a Broken Soul Tarot is a richly gothic deck in generally highly contrasting, and is the indication of craftsman Ash's shadow work. This 22 card constrained release is accessible from Adam McLean, and there is likewise now an entire 78 card version.

Dracula Tarot Open

The Dracula Tarot has 78 cards dependent on Bram Stoker's renowned novel, Dracula. The major arcana highlight characters from the book, while the minor arcana follow key storylines. The deck and friend book have been independently published by the writer.

Mythical beast Age Inquisition Tarot

The Dragon Age Inquisition Tarot is a completely delineated 78 card deck dependent on the characters and fine art of the pretending computer game of a similar name. While it's basically for fanatics of the game, the deck has some tarot foundation. As of now just accessible packaged in an exceptional release of the computer game.

Dreams and Nightmares - Oracle of the Night

Dreams and Nightmares - Oracle of the Night is a 108-card deck motivated by shamanic ventures

Pixie Tarot Decks

Pixie Tarot and Oracle cards and decks with pictures of pixies, faeries, the fae and nature spirits.

Faerie Enchantments Oracle

The Faerie Enchantments Oracle is a 40-card deck dependent on Celtic magick and imagery, and represented with Faerie energies, goddesses and divine beings. It's intended for making your very own charms, so the backs of the cards have supernatural correspondences and data.

Faerie Guidance Oracle

The Faerie Guidance Oracle is a 40-card deck intended for individual and profound improvement. It's from Paulina Cassidy, from the maker of the Paulina Tarot, and is shown in her mark style.

Faerie Tarot

The Faerie Tarot is a tremendously bright, eccentric and positive deck of 78 fae cards. There's an obscure likeness to Rider-Waite in certain cards, yet most cards take their own representative course. Every individual card additionally has a contrastingly planned outskirt in the shades of the card. Appropriate for more established kids and adolescents, and the youthful on the most fundamental level.

Faeries Oracle

Bring an excursion into Faeryland and its lovely scenes of mythical beings, imps, trolls, and obviously, faeries. Computerized pictures don't do the Faeries Oracle deck equity.

Faery Wicca Tarot

Gain proficiency with the stories and legends of Old Ireland in the Faery Wicca Tarot. In view of the cutting edge Faery convention of the nature based Wiccan religion, the fine art is brilliant with essential hues yet rather alluring.

Pixie Lenormand Oracle

The Fairy Lenormand Oracle is a huge size, 36-card Lenormand deck with a dream pixie topic. The cards have smooth, point by point outlines of lovely pixies in a storybook world.

Pixie Lights Tarot

The Fairy Lights Tarot has 78 inventive dream cards, made from 39 unique compositions - each card is half of a greater picture. The deck is from a similar craftsman as the Tarot of the Secret Forest.

Pixie Ring Oracle

The Fairy Ring Oracle is the wonderful second deck from the makers of the Sacred Circle Tarot. This one depends on British and Irish pixie legends and has fours suits of fourteen cards and eight 'pixie celebration' cards.

Pixie Tarot

The Fairy Tarot is a charming Italian deck with a solid dream impact. The 78 capricious cards show captivating scenes of fun loving pixies and timberland animals.

Pixie Tarot Cards

The Fairy Tarot Cards is an entire 78-card tarot from Doreen Virtue, with point by point old-style pixie fine art by artist Howard David Johnson. There is certain, ace dynamic knowledge at the base of every one of the 78 cards, and a definite 185-page partner manual is remembered for the set.

Pixie Tarot Mini

The Fairy Tarot Mini is the pocket-sized, scaled down release of the adorable and beguiling Fairy Tarot from Antonio Lupatelli. The 78 cards are unusual and include dwarves, pixies, mythical people and sylphs.

Fey Tarot

A ravishing and one of a kind tarot of the Fey, not the British pixies, yet a progressively all-inclusive assortment portrayed in craftsmanship with an anime feel. The Fey Tarot is a well-considered and painstakingly structured tarot set for peruser everything being equal - and a lovely, fun loving deck loaded with its own novel enchantment.

Timberland Folklore Tarot

The Forest Folklore Tarot is roused by the New Forest, an antiquated forest in England. The mixed watercolor and photographic cards include woods natural life and pixies, dwarves and fairies from legend.

Mending with the Faeries

By Doreen Virtue, creator of a few prophet decks, the Healing with the Faeries Oracle is a non-tarot deck has beautiful pictures of pixies and a solitary word or expression to summarize on each card.

Heart of Faerie Oracle

The Heart of Faerie Oracle is a 68-card deck of the fae from Brian and Wendy Fraud. Brian is the maker of the Faerie Oracle and the renowned Pressed Fairy Book, and Wendy made dolls in The Dark Crystal.

Helices Tarot

The Helices Tarot is a unique pixie themed deck, which was hand-painted in delicate however point by point water hues. The craftsman has followed the Rider-Waite convention so as to make it simple for learners. This delightful, borderless, mysterious deck is presently finished and accessible in a quality independently published version with a bound 56-page book.

Moving Wisdom from Angels and Fairies

The Inspirational Wisdom from Angels and Fairies deck has 44 iridescent cards detonating with shading, each including beautiful pictures of pale and young pixies and blessed messengers. Each card has a positive message of direction going with the picture

Keijuoraakkeli

Keijuoraakkeli is a Finnish-distributed Fairy Oracle deck of 44 cards. The somewhat beautiful acrylic-painted cards are partitioned into the four seasons, which symbolize life's excursion. The deck and booklet is in Finnish, yet is accessible with a flyer converted into English.

Le Carte delgi Elfi

Another Celtic Oracle Deck, le Carte degli Elfi highlights faeries in glowing, cloudy pastel watercolors. In spite of the Italian title of the deck, the card titles are for the most part in English.

Enchanted Messages from the Fairies

The Magical Messages from the Fairies Oracle is a 44 -card prophet from Doreen Virtue. Each card in the deck includes a 'nature holy messenger' - a pixie - and a message. Reasonable for youngsters or grown -ups.

Messages from the Wee Folk

The Messages from the Wee Folk set is intended to assist you with associating with the Wee Folk and the hallowed energies of nature. Notwithstanding the name, the pictures have something other than pixies - there are blossoms, creepy crawlies, dolphins and the sky is the limit from there. The set has 33 cards and a huge 229-page partner book.

Spiritualist Faerie Tarot

The Mystic Faerie Tarot is a captivating faerie tarot painted in watercolors by dream craftsman Linda Ravenscroft. Lavish fringes and gold edges encompass tarot pictures of sprites, fairies, mermaids and faeries, in a beguiling, pretty and lucid new tarot deck.

Prophet of the Dragonfae

The Oracle of the Dragonfae has 43 cards with rather beautiful outlines of goddesses, divine beings, mythical beasts, winged fitures and fantastical characters. It is ascribed to Australian deck maker, Lucy Cavendish, however really has cards contributed by seven unique craftsmen.

Otherworld Tarot

The Otherworld Tarot has been enlivened by pixie craftsman, Sarah Nowell. The major arcana cards are improved, however brilliant and alluring. The minors wander from the Rider-Waite scenes, depending more on the suit tokens and a couple of items to pass on the tarot meaning.

Paulina Tarot

The Paulina Tarot fabricates a supernatural, capricious normal world through its 78 cards. Paulina Cassidy's aesthetic style is unimaginably multifaceted and loaded with detail, shaded with watercolor washes in quieted tints. It's somewhat Victorian, a little Tim Burton-esque, and exceptionally captivating.

Soul of Flowers Tarot

A sweet and adorable tarot of blossoms, set in a lush fantasy world. Each card in the Spirit of Flowers Tarot has a practically drawn bloom and a small, honest pixie related with it.

Tarot of the Celtic Fairies

The Tarot of Celtic Fairies is a lot of fey knowledge and direction, with 78 cards and a manual composed by Mark McElroy. "Excursion to a hauntingly delightful fairie land saturated with Celtic legend. Striking, luminescent scenes vibrate with huge detail, profound significance, and sheer excellence."

Tarot of the Hidden Realm

The Tarot of the Hidden Realm has 78 expressive, fascinating, and borderless pictures. Instead of depending on customary tarot images, it strips back its pictures to the crude components of nature and the fae. The workmanship is brimming with life, development and feeling.

Tarot of the Magical Forest

The Tarot of the Magical Forest is a peculiar excursion through a universe of abnormal yet adorable creatures and characters in eye-getting Rider-Waite based representations. First distributed in Taiwan by Taiwanese craftsman Leo Tang, it's likewise been re-distributed by Lo Scarabeo with their standard outskirts.

Tarot of the Nymphs

The Tarot of the Nymphs speaks to the 78 cards through the paradigms of the Nymphs, female nature spirits connected with water and youth. The cards are delineated in watercolor, with alluring and erotic pictures of sparsely clad, physically impeccable sprites.

Tarot of the Secret Forest

The Tarot of the Secret Forest is a one of a kind deck with dream timberland scenes on the two sides of the cards. The essences of the cards have the scene in shading, while the back shows it in highly contrasting.

Tarot of the Sidhe

The Tarot of the Sidhe has 78 cards with unique, vivid Faerie compositions. It was sold-out as a majors-just set from Adam McLean, and has now likewise been distributed as an entire 78-card deck by Schiffer Books.

Tarots of the Golden Dawn

The Tarots of the Golden Dawn is a deck highlighting mythical people and pixie type figures - certainly not a mysterious Tarot

Feline Tarot Decks

Feline Tarot decks, prophets and cards of the catlike influence, about or including felines.

Extravagant Bohemian Cats' Tarot

The Baroque Bohemian Cats' Tarot is unique. Three components: genuine felines everything being equal and breeds, beautiful Baroque ensembles, and an extravagant European condition, have been carefully mixed into a serviceable Tarot deck for all feline darlings.

Dark Cats Tarot

The Black Cats Tarot is another cat roused deck, this one concentrating on the mysterious dark feline. The 78 cards blend dream and reality in its picture of human-like dark felines.

Bleu Cat Tarot

The Bleu Cat Tarot has 78 cards with somewhat unique pictures of a fun loving and human Siamese feline, delineated in blue. From Beth Seilonen, craftsman of the Dream Raven Tarot and Tarot of

Leaves, and propelled by perceptions of her own Siamese feline.

Feline Wisdom Cards

The Cat Wisdom prophet deck has 45 very adorable cards with a catchphrase beside studio photographs of cushioned cats in different stances. The partner booklet has light uplifting counsel.

Feline's Eye Tarot

The Cat's Eye Tarot is by a catlike veterinarian, an individual extremely acquainted with felines, their propensities and characters. These felines are exceptionally characteristic and genuine, but have been wonderfully adjusted to Tarot cards. The deck is currently finished and distributed by US Games.

Felines Inspirational Oracle

The Cats Inspirational Oracle has 32 distinct types of felines on its 32 cards. The cards have consistent with life delineations of each breed, and connection their run of the mill conduct with a card catchphrase: the Turkish Van is swimming

(Boldness), the Burmese looking for consideration (Attention), the Maine Coon chasing (Pursue). The set accompanies a buddy book by Barbara Moore.

CatTarot

The CatTarot is a remarkable 78-card deck of cats outlined as renowned figures from writing, history, TV and motion pictures. The cast of characters is differing, from Marilyn Monroe to Genghis Khan to Captain Nemo to Luke Skywalker. An enchanting, clever, and wonderfully delineated tarot deck.

Visit du Marseille Tarot

The Chat du Marseilles Tarot is a trumps-just deck attracted French style, in view of the 1761 Conver Marseilles. It's very conventional however for a certain something - rather than people, there are felines!

I Gatti

The Gatti deck is an Italian Tarot of 22 cards, each including a feline outlined in highly contrasting. It's the feline rendition of the I Cani deck, additionally by Menegazzi, and is a restricted release with unlaminated and somewhat contrastingly measured cards.

Kissatarot

The Kissatarot is a Finnish tarot deck, which interprets as the 'CatTarot'. It's a quiet inclination deck represented in a vivid, 'credulous' style, where enigmatic felines now and again supplant the human figures on the cards, and are now and then notwithstanding them.

Marseille Cat Tarot

The Marseille Cat Tarot cheerfully consolidates the verifiable French tarot custom and human felines, with different textured cats instead of the human characters on the cards. The deck is shown with solid essential hues, yet more refined work of art than the customary woodcut prints. The minor arcana likewise have little cat scenes in the midst of the pips.

Medieval Cat Tarot

The Medieval Cat Tarot is an exquisite deck of privileged cats in Renaissance dress and style. The 78 cards have customary roots yet have been refreshed and rearranged in imagery, making it reasonable for novices and the more experienced peruser.

Mysterious Cats Tarot

The Mystical Cats Tarot has 78 borderless pictures outlined with practically drawn felines carrying on as felines do - simply inside tarot scenes. It's a delight to see typical felines (not dressed or in human-like situations) with cat non-verbal communication coordinated to the inclination and significance of every tarot card.

Taro Gatti

I Taro Gatti is a 22-card Italian deck, from a paper organization in Perugia. Felines are the topic and have likewise become the Tarot images in a few cards. The work of art is dark, white and red imprinted on thick, solid uncoated cardboard and is very engaging.

Tarot Cat-a-Vasya

The Tarot Cat-a-Vasya is an enjoyment and kitschy photograph collaged deck of felines. The Russian-distributed deck has 80 cards with every unique breed and sorts of felines as the characters in tarot scenes.

Tarot du Chat

This is a 78 card French Tarot dedicated to, what else, felines! The tarot scenes in the Tarot du Chat are European style, and rather than people they highlight ordinary and anthropomorphised felines.

Tarot for Cats

The Tarot for Cats shows felines rather than people to outline the cards, of which there is just the major arcana. The Hanging Cat is a specific most loved of mine... I could pretty much edge these cards.

Tarot of Pagan Cats

The Tarot of Pagan Cats sees the tarot from a feline's eye see. In view of the Rider-Waite imagery, the agnostic association is inconspicuous and the cards show felines acting as characteristic cats in well-known tarot scenes.

Tarot of Pagan Cats Mini

The Tarot of Pagan Cats Mini is the small scale version of the full size Tarot of Pagan Cats. It's an effectively convenient rendition of the extremely adorable yet entirely coherent 78 card deck.

Tarot of the Cat People

Felines all things considered, including lions and panthers, go with the bright Cat People in this deck for every one of those feline darlings out there. The fine art in the Tarot of the Cat People is delightfully done.

Tarot of the White Cats

The Tarot of the White Cats is especially in the convention of the Rider-Waite Tarot - with the exception of the blue-peered toward, white felines attracted the cards, rather than individuals. The imagery is standard and non-undermining enough for use for the Tarot learner.

Tarot of White Cats Mini

Tarot of White Cats Mini is the little size form of the Tarot of White Cats, a smaller than usual deck intended to fit in a pocket or handbag. The 78 cards depend intently on the Rider-Waite deck however outlined with white cats in an assortment of positions.

Agnostic and Wiccan Tarot Decks

Tarot cards and prophet decks for Wiccans, Pagans and Witches, in light of the nature religions and otherworldliness of Wicca, Paganism and Witchcraft.

Chemist's Spell Tarot

The Alchemist's Spell Tarot is a piece of the Complete Wish Granting Kit, which is intended for clairvoyant tarot readings related to 154 spells. The 22 staggering major arcana cards accompany a rundown of spells on the backs.

Book of Shadows Tarot

The Book of Shadows Tarot is the principal volume in a two volume deck set conceptualized by tarot master, Barbara Moore. This is the 'as above' deck, concentrating on general and awesome energies, while the subsequent will be 'so underneath' and focus on ordinary human encounters.

Book of Shadows Tarot: Volume 2

This Book of Shadows Tarot is the second deck in the exceptional two volume Book of Shadows unit. This is the 'So Below' deck, focusing on the supernatural energies that encompass us in regular day to day existence.

Chrysalis Tarot

The Chrysalis Tarot is a 78-card deck of brilliant, point by point artworks with a Pagan vibe and rich imagery from creator Toney Brooks and craftsman Holly Sierra. A wonderful and exceptional independent deck, it takes another and non-conventional way to deal with tarot, with new paradigms in the majors and new outlines in the minors and court cards.

Regular Witch Tarot

The Everyday Witch Tarot has 78 unconventional tarot scenes of dark hatted witches approaching their lives, set in a universe of medieval dream blended in with present day reality. It's an enchanting deck of positive energies, genuine goal, and light heart.

Faery Wicca Tarot

Become familiar with the stories and legends of Old Ireland in the Faery Wicca Tarot. In light of the cutting edge Faery convention of the nature based Wiccan religion, the work of art is splendid with essential hues but instead alluring.

Association of the Fool Tarot

The Fellowship of the Fool Tarot has 78 lavish and enthusiastic watercolor cards, mirroring the life of and universes went by the craftsman. The deck mixes Paganism and domain of imagination with 21st century life. It's been independently published and is accessible from the craftsman.

Gaian Tarot

The Gaian Tarot is a Schiffer Books version of Joanna Powell Colbert's advanced, comprehensive, regular world based 78-card deck. This version has huge cards, silver edging and a re-altered friend book - just as Joanna's wonderful unique representations.

Glastonbury Tarot

The Glastonbury Tarot is a blend of Arthurian, Pagan and Christian impact, and the fantasies, history, customs and inhabitants of the community/hallowed site of Glastonbury, England, structure the premise of this splendidly shaded tarot deck.

Green Witch Tarot

The Green Witch Tarot is a lovely 78-card deck dependent on nature-based Paganism. It has astute, pleasant and borderless cards that have been re-deciphered around green black magic, yet are still effectively coherent. The cards accompany a point by point 240-page friend manual.

Jolanda Tarot

The Jolanda Tarot is a reproduce of the Swedish Witch Tarot, named after the magickal name of the maker, Jolanda cave Tredjes. This variant has purple rather than dark fringes around the line workmanship outlines.

Present day Spellcaster's Tarot

The Modern Spellcaster's Tarot is a comprehensive, multicultural 78-card deck of Pagan imagery in a blend of current, medieval and dream outlines. It's structured explicitly for use in magickal practice and spell work, just as for reflection and tarot readings.

Agnostic Lenormand Oracle

The Pagan Lenormand Oracle is the main Pagan arranged Lenormand deck, where the customary images have been re-deciphered to show Pagan decent variety, symbology and convictions. It's from Gina Pace, who additionally made the Pagan Tarot.

Agnostic Otherworlds Tarot

The Pagan Otherworlds Tarot is an excellent deck in each angle, from fine art to the printing quality. It has 84 cards - it incorporates one additional major arcana and five novel 'Luna' cards - with save yet amazing representations with the vibe of Renaissance craftsmanship.

Agnostic Tarot

The Pagan (Tarot 2000) is a Pagan tarot deck for the new thousand years, distributed in Cornwall, England in 2000. The card fine art is a hand painted and very bustling style with an outskirt of Celtic knotwork.

Agnostic Tarot

The Pagan Tarot, from Gina M. Pace (known as Wicce on the Internet), joins the delights and issues of regular day to day existence with Wiccan and Pagan otherworldliness. The craftsmanship shows Pagan scenes and is likewise present day and ultra-reasonable: PCs highlight in a few cards.

Agnostic Tarot Mini

The Pagan Tarot Mini is the small scale variant of Gina M. Pace's Pagan Tarot. The 78 cards have representations extending from the cutting edge and contemporary to Pagan and Wiccan imagery.

Agnostic Ways Tarot

The Pagan Ways Tarot is a 78-card tarot made around the Pagan perspective, otherworldliness, images and gods. Its pictures are photographically based, including genuine individuals on themed foundations. The deck is from Anna Franklin, a Pagan priestess who likewise made the prior Sacred Circle Tarot.

Robin Wood Tarot

Simple for novices and tarot newcomers to use with its Rider-Waite establishment, Robin Wood's self-titled Tarot deck is additionally wealthy in Pagan imagery. The representations in this well-known deck are appealing, and splendidly yet not brutally shaded.

Consecrated Circle Tarot

In view of the Celtic Pagan point of view, the Sacred Circle Tarot utilizes photos of hallowed locales, just as customary plant and creature relationship from Ancient Britain. The fine art is a blend of hand drawings, photography, and PC produced pictures which don't generally mix well, yet by and large the deck is very enchanting.

Erotic Wicca Tarot

The Sensual Wicca Tarot investigates sex and sexuality through the Wiccan conviction framework. The card outlines by and large have a Rider-Waite establishment, rethought to be multicultural and Wicca. Only one out of every odd card has suggestive symbolism, however of those that do, be cautioned - some almost be X evaluated.

Shapeshifter Tarot

Shapeshifting is the taking on of creature character during daze. The Shapeshifter Tarot is a flawlessly mysterious and expressive deck from a capable craftsman, delineating a framework with its foundations in Paganism and European shamanism.

Silver Witchcraft Tarot

The Silver Witchcraft Tarot blends tarot with present day agnostic imagery and magickal understanding. Represented in profound, air shading, it has a multicultural cast of robed characters set in great nature-based scenes. The 78 borderless cards are upgraded by silver metallic edges, and there's additionally a friend book by Barbara Moore.

Tarot de las Brujas

El Tarot de las Brujas is a Spanish deck (the title interprets as the Tarot of the Witches). It has 28 cards, 21 of which compare to the major arcana, and the other 7 show devices regular to Witchcraft and are sprinkled through different majors.

Tarot Familiars

The Tarot Familiars is a 78-card deck of creatures in otherworldly settings, by natural life craftsman Lisa Parker. The major arcana and court cards well describe every creature, however tragically the minor arcana cards are unillustrated pip cards.

Tarot for Hip Witches

The Tarot for Hip Witches is an energetic 78-card deck and book set loaded with youthful and excellent witches. The tarot pictures from the Witchy Tarot are brilliant, vivid and to some degree non-conventional. There is additionally a little friend book.

Tarot of Pagan Cats

The Tarot of Pagan Cats sees the tarot from a feline's eye see. In light of the Rider-Waite imagery, the agnostic association is unobtrusive and the cards show felines carrying on as normal cats in well-known tarot scenes.

Tarot of Pagan Cats Mini

The Tarot of Pagan Cats Mini is the scaled down version of the full size Tarot of Pagan Cats. It's an effectively versatile variant of the exceptionally charming however truly discernible 78 card deck.

Tarot of the Druids

The Tarot of the Druids is enlivened by antiquated Irish customs and divinities, and Celtic life and culture. The pictures are silly and fairly diverting.

Tarot of the Old Path

The Tarot of the Old Path draws on various social viewpoints and is proposed for Pagan Tarot perusers. Surely understood Wiccans, the Farrars and Margot Adler, likewise helped the makers.

Tarot of Wicca

Distributed in Japan however titled in English, the cards of the Tarot of Wicca are a PC created style and have an accentuation on the human structure.

The Gospel of Aradia

The Gospel of Aradia is a prophet of 34 cards based around the lessons of Aradia, an adored Italian Witch. The deck has a premise in Stregoneria yet is comprehensive to present day Pagans, Wiccans and Witches.

Waking the Wild Spirit Tarot

The Waking the Wild Spirit Tarot is a capricious, non-conventional deck.

Goddess Tarot Decks

Prophets and Tarot cards and decks highlighting goddesses and female and ladylike divinities.

AboraMana

AboraMana is a lot of Goddess knowledge cards, the symbolism and arrangement of which were naturally diverted by the craftsman. The 89 cards are not tarot or a prophet deck, however portrayed as a represented cosmology, that clarifies 'the human situation in the stupendous plan of creation... from a solely lady's perspective'.

Native Goddess Chakra Cards

The Aboriginal Goddess Chakra Cards were enlivened by the association between the creator's Australian native otherworldliness, the chakras, and divinities from different societies. It has 49 cards with also mixed representations.

Antiquated Feminine Wisdom

The 'Antiquated Feminine Wisdom of Goddesses and Heroines Divination Deck' (to give its full title) is a 52 card set, from the makers of the Celestial Tarot. Each appealing card includes a female character delineated in a full scene, with her name above and a watchword beneath.

Dull Goddess Tarot

The Dark Goddess Tarot highlights 78 goddesses and legendary ladies, figures who may be viewed as dull, shadow or testing. The unmistakable, striking workmanship is outwardly predictable, yet remains consistent with every goddess' sources. It's a profound and well-made deck, independently published in a restricted version of 1000 duplicates.

Gaia Oracle

The Gaia Oracle includes the work of art of Toni Carmine Salerno on its 45 cards. The deck is motivated by Gaia, the Earth goddess, and offers mending and direction through its specialty and assertions.

Goddess Guidance Oracle

The Goddess Guidance Oracle has 44 lovely cards for ladylike direction, including goddesses from around the globe from Mother Mary to Kali.

Goddess Inspiration Oracle

The Goddess Inspiration Oracle is a 80-card deck from skilled craftsman Kris Waldherr, maker of the Goddess Tarot. The workmanship shows 80 goddesses from differing societies and conventions, and both surely understood and lesser known divinities.

Goddess Knowledge Cards

The Goddess Knowledge Cards isn't carefully a tarot or Oracle Deck, yet a lovely arrangement of 48 cards portraying goddesses from societies around the globe. Center Eastern, Chinese, Scandinavian, Egyptian just as Greek and Roman pantheons are spoken to, all painted in otherworldly and splendid style.

Goddess in a hurry

The Goddess in a hurry pack is a little deck of 33 elevating compositions of ladies moving and in a hurry, connected with a heart-focused certifiable expression. From Amy Sophia Marashinsky, maker of the Goddess Oracle, and craftsman Melissa Harris.

Goddess Oracle

The Goddess Oracle from Thalia Took is a straightforward deck of eighty-one cards, each delineating an alternate female divinities from everywhere throughout the world. The aesthetic style is solid and unmistakable, not cutesy, and perfectly hued. Still in progress.

Goddess Oracle

The Goddess Oracle is a wonderful deck that consolidates pictures of Goddesses from societies around the globe, with Goddess verse, custom and folklore to be utilized for direction and understanding and well as a prophet.

Goddess Tarot

One of my top choices, the Goddess Tarot deck consolidates Goddess pictures and legend from numerous societies into an extremely excellent and well-made Tarot deck of 78 cards.

Goddesses and Sirens Oracle

The Goddesses and Sirens Oracle praises the Feminine Divine, with 38 cards of goddesses and ladies of folklore, and a buddy book of spells and summons and the history behind every Goddess. It's the corresponding deck to the Gods and Titans Oracle.

GoddessGuides Intuition Cards

The GoddessGuides Intuition Cards are the production of craftsman, Glen Ladegaard, who represents considerable authority in the female naked. One side of the cards highlights one of Glen's Sacred Feminine Goddesses and on the other, her own uplifting reflections. Accessible in English just as Spanish.

Hekate Tarot

The Hekate Tarot started as a reverential venture to respect the goddess Hekate by two of her priestesses and fans. Their total deck has 66 cards with blended media outlines, and incorporates 26 majors and 40 suit cards, however excludes the court cards.

I Ching of the Goddess

The I Ching of the Goddess consolidates women's activist otherworldliness and innovativeness; the Eastern arrangement of divination, the I Ching; and the craftsmanship of Barbara Walker in its 64 cards. The cards have the I Ching images, an aesthetic scene and logical watchwords on each card.

Isis Oracle

The Isis Oracle has 44 cards motivated by the secrets of the Ancient Egyptian goddess, Isis, to help the peruser on the way towards otherworldly dominance. The partner book contains guided contemplations, ceremonies and representations to extend the effect of the cards.

Excursion Cards

The Journey Cards include multicultural goddesses and up 'til now obscure female holy people that were envisioned by the craftsman. This divination deck of 55 cards has multifaceted pen-and-ink drawings, and is intended for 'direction, revelations, and disclosures'. The set is independently published and furthermore accompanies a 132-page manual.

Excursion to the Goddess Realm Oracle

The Journey to the Goddess Realm Oracle has 39 cards devoted to goddesses and female divinities from around the globe. This female deck of happy and itemized cards has an advanced vibe and is intended to help with ordinary choices and day by day direction.

Kuan Yin Oracle

The Kuan Yin Oracle has 44 beautiful cards themed around the vitality of Kuan Yin, the Chinese goddess of empathy, unlimited love and acknowledgment. The deck of direction and positive, reasonable and otherworldly counsel is joined by a 144-page manual by Alana Fairchild.

Legendary Goddess Tarot

The Mythical Goddess Tarot is intended to assist you with understanding your Sacred Feminine Essence, through access to the numerous essences of the Goddess. It's a non-standard deck of 78 cards, with pictures that are energetic and loaded with vitality.

Prophet of the Goddess

The Oracle of the Goddess set from Sylvie Winter and Jo Dose (not to be mistaken for the numerous different decks of a similar name) has 33 alluring cards with goddess models. It's fundamentally the same as in look to the Vision Quest Tarot, from similar makers.

CPSIA information can be obtained
at www.ICGtesting.com
Printed in the USA
LVHW080447280421
685801LV00016B/1737

9 781801 385268